everyday
tidiness

everyday tidiness

365 WAYS TO A DECLUTTERED LIFE

Bounty
BOOKS

An Hachette UK Company
www.hachette.co.uk

First published in 2016 by Bounty Books,
a division of Octopus Publishing Group Ltd
Carmelite House
50 Victoria Embankment
London, EC4Y 0DZ
www.octopusbooks.co.uk

Copyright © Octopus Publishing Group Ltd 2016

ISBN: 978-0-7537-3114-7

A CIP catalogue record for this book is available
from the British Library

Printed and bound in China

10 9 8 7 6 5 4 3 2

Publisher: Lucy Pessell
Design Manager: Megan van Staden
Design: Wide Open Studio
Contributing Editor: Emma Hill
Editor: Natalie Bradley
Production Manager: Caroline Alberti
Images: Shutterstock/Irtsya

INTRODUCTION

Tidy (verb):
*Bring order to;
arrange neatly*

Are you tired of losing track of your keys every time you put them down? Do you have a decade's worth of paperwork stashed away somewhere? Are you struggling to reach the bottom of your laundry basket? Is your closet bursting at the seams? If so, don't despair, *Everyday Tidiness* provides a tidying tip, a decluttering exercise or inspirational quote for every day of the year.

These simple tidiness techniques will help you to create and maintain a clean and orderly home that's a joy to live in; decluttering advice will provide inspiration to ditch those things you really don't need in your life and enhance those that you do, while clever storage hacks will enable you to make the most of the room that you have. And if you think achieving a tidy home transforms only your space, think again. The act of creating order from chaos is incredibly beneficial to our mental health and happiness levels.

Getting rid of the things that we don't need, that we may have been clutching on to for misguided sentimental reasons, can be incredibly cathartic. The act of decluttering has the ability to generate fresh energy, create both mental and physical space, and release negative emotions.

So use this book as your guide, inspiration, and motivation to embrace a simpler life; streamline your possessions, develop time-saving tidying habits and gain clarity and focus. Make this the year you take control of your home environment and your life.

WHERE TO START?

Select one area, clear it and make this your no-clutter zone. It can be your dining room table, a kitchen counter, your bedroom floor — wherever you start, make a rule: nothing can be placed there that's not actually in use. Everything must be put away. Once you have that clutter-free zone, keep it that way. Now, each day slowly expand your no-clutter zone until it envelops the whole house.

"Owning less is better than organizing more."

– JOSHUA BECKER

TIDY DESK,
TIDY MIND

Whatever else may be happening in your office space, keep your desk free of all but essential items. There is something about having a clean work area that makes us more productive and frees our mind to concentrate on the task at hand. How many times have you been working on a project only to find yourself glancing at papers on your desk? And so your mind wanders to the contents of those papers…

"In the scope of a happy life, a messy desk or an overstuffed coat closet is a trivial thing, yet I find — and I hear from other people that they agree — that getting rid of clutter gives a disproportionate boost to happiness."

– GRETCHEN RUBIN

MAKE YOUR BED

Each and every day make your bed before you leave the bedroom. Your bed is likely the largest thing in the room, so if this is tidy it will in turn make the room look tidy. Getting into a made bed has also been said to encourage a better night's sleep, so it's a win-win.

PUT THINGS AWAY

Such a simple one — put things away after using them.
Yes, everything. If there's no room for something, throw out
something else you haven't used in a while to make way for it.

"A place for everything, and everything in its place."

– MRS BEETON

TIDY BY CATEGORY

Try the KonMari method and tidy by category, not room, in the following order: clothes, books, papers, miscellaneous items, and sentimental items. Marie Kondo believes that by following this order, you'll be able to properly detect whether an item "sparks joy" by the time you roll around to the more important items, such as photos or mementos.

MULTITASK

Clean the shower while you're taking a shower. Soak dishes in the sink while you are eating dinner. This will cut back the time you have to dedicate to cleaning.

STORAGE HACK #1

Nowhere to dry your clothes? Hang a ladder – painted in an attractive color – from your ceiling and use coat hangers to hang your wet clothes to dry.

KEEP YOUR DINING ROOM TABLE CLEAR

Dining room tables tend to be magnets for clutter. Keep the surface completely free of knick-knacks and it's less likely to become a catch-all for "floating" items such as keys, mail, bags, and much more.

"Clear clutter.
Make space
for you."

– MAGDALENA VANDENBERG

"For a happier
life keep only the
things you
love and use."

– SELIM TOLGA

CLEAR UNDER THE BED

If you're in the habit of "tidying" things away under the bed, now is the time to stop. It's too easy for items to disappear under there and for the dust to collect. Instead of using this space as a hiding place, clear it out and keep it free of clutter. You will be amazed at how clearing things you thought were hidden can transform the light and space of a room.

"Clutter is not just the stuff on your floor — it's anything that stands between you and the life you want to be living."

– PETER WALSH

STORAGE HACK #2

Use clip coat hangers to store tall boots. They can be hung from a custom-made line or curtain pole fixed into your closet.

ORGANIZE YOUR RECIPES

Keep all of your cook books in one place. Flag up the pages featuring your favorite recipes with sticky tabs. Go one step further and use different colored tabs to categorize (for example, family meals, entertaining, and lunches). If you have any loose recipes from magazines or on paper, sort them into a binder.

"Organizing is what you do before you do something, so that when you do it, it is not all mixed up."

– WINNIE THE POOH

"For every minute spent organizing, an hour is earned."

– BENJAMIN FRANKLIN

ADD SPARKLE

Why not string up fairy lights in a room you've recently revamped through tidying? It's a great way to add extra sparkle to a spick-and-span room.

"You may have occasion to possess or use material things, but the secret of life lies in never missing them."

– GANDHI

"The most important things in life aren't things."

– ANTHONY J. D'ANGELO

A LITTLE EACH DAY

If the idea of decluttering your entire house in one mammoth tidying session is too overwhelming, tackle small tasks each day.

"The best way to get something done is to begin."

– UNKNOWN

SAVOR TIDINESS

Today, wherever you have managed to tidy — whether it is an entire room or just a small area — savor that tidiness you have created. Take a deep breath and enjoy the serene feeling of having brought order to chaos.

"Cleanliness makes it easier to see the details."

— ANIEKEE TOCHUKWU EZEKIEL

LEAVE NO TRACE

This is a mindfulness exercise that will help you to live both in a more peaceful state and a more pleasant environment. As messiness levels rise, often so do anxiety levels. We then swoop in and tidy in a state of annoyance, but what if we never created any mess in the first place? OK, this ambition may be too high for all but the Zen masters among us, but we can take some steps toward achieving this through a simple exercise. Today, select one room in your house and for one week try to leave no trace that you've used that space. If you choose the kitchen, for example, wash crockery as you use it; wipe down any spills from the sides; put everything back in the cabinets. Clean up in such a way that it looks as though you were never there.

THE THREE-THINGS RULE

Each time you walk into a room in your house pick up three things from the floor/the sides and put them in their right place before you get on with what you were doing.

"A messy room equals a messy mind."

– MARIE KONDO

SET BOUNDARIES

Determine how much is enough and stay within that boundary.
Are two pairs of jeans enough or are three? Setting boundaries
will help to ensure that excess items in your home don't build up.

"Simplicity is making the journey of this life with just baggage enough."

– UNKNOWN

BATHROOM CABINET

Tackle your bathroom cabinet, closets, and shelves today. Throw away any beauty products that have been open for years (and possibly save yourself from a nasty rash), expired medicines, blunt razors, used tubes of toothpastes, that luxurious product you couldn't quite bring yourself to throw out because there's 0.002 ml left in the bottom. Remove anything that isn't either essential to your everyday washing routine (toothpaste, shampoo, soap) or joyous (indulgent bath oil, an extravagant perfume, glittery body mousse).

STORAGE HACK #3

Attach a magnetic strip to the inside of your medicine cabinet to store bobby pins, nail clippers, tweezers, and other small metal objects.

"Tidiness is a virtue, symmetry is often a constituent of beauty."

– WINSTON CHURCHILL

CREATE EMAIL FOLDERS

Don't neglect digital clear outs — it's not just our homes that get cluttered. Inboxes can become overwhelmed with junk and entirely disorganized if we don't keep a handle on them. Create folders for all areas of your life — work clients, doctors, parent mail — so you can easily locate emails when you need to. When the project or year is over, delete!

"Being organized isn't about getting rid of everything you own or trying to become a different person; it's about living the way you want to live, but better."

– ANDREW MELLEN

REWARD YOUR EFFORTS

If you manage to clear out an area that was always cluttered —
your closet, "that" drawer, whatever it may be — make sure you
reward yourself for your efforts. Take a moment to indulge in a
cup of tea/a cake/a sit down — whatever floats your boat.
Do the same each time you tackle a tricky area of your house.
Give yourself an incentive to tidy.

"You can't reach
for anything new
if your hands
are still full of
yesterday's junk."

– LOUISE SMITH

"Use it up,
wear it out,
make it do,
or do without."

— NEW ENGLAND PROVERB

ORGANIZE YOUR KITCHEN UTENSILS

Why not store kitchenware by task? For example, all baking supplies in one drawer, pots and pans in another, and knives and cutting tools elsewhere.

"Hard work is often the easy work you did not do at the proper time."

– BERNARD METZLER

GO PAPERLESS

Utility companies and banks now offer the option to go paperless. Doing this is a really transformative step in clearing the clutter. Paperwork can become overwhelming and is often just shoved into a drawer or closet never to be looked at again. Banish this with one click of a box and save a few trees in the process.

"Paper clutter is no more than postponed decisions."

– BARBARA HEMPHILL

STORAGE HACK #4

Don't hide your most-used kitchen accessories deep in a drawer. Get quick access by hanging them on an easy-to-install dowel rod.

MAKE AN ENTRANCE

Your hall or foyer is the last thing you see when you leave the house and the first thing you see when you return, so make an effort to keep this area clutter free and attractive. Use decorative hooks as a place to keep your keys, purse, and any other items that would otherwise be dumped on the nearest available surface as you walk through the door.

Designate a home for all your possessions and avoid wasting time looking for them. Research shows that we lose up to nine items every day – or 198,743 in a lifetime. Phones, keys, sunglasses, and paperwork top the list.

BEDSIDE SPACE

Creating bedside space will not only improve the overall look of your bedroom, it will aid a good night's sleep. Remove any piled up books, water glasses or anything else from the bedside. Permit yourself a night table (with entirely clear surfaces) and a lamp. A more minimalist sleeping area will help you to tune out the day's distractions more effectively.

"Organizing is making space for the things that we love and use the most. Simplifying is letting go of those things that we don't love and will rarely or never use."

– LESLIE HOYT

REARRANGE YOUR FURNITURE

Rearranging your furniture can make a space feel new and uncluttered. Focus on keeping clear pathways and a good flow throughout the house as well as ensuring nothing is blocking light coming through the windows.

USE MIRRORS

Consider putting up an extra mirror or two in place of a picture. This will make your walls look less busy and create the illusion of more space.

CULL YOUR SHOE COLLECTION

Have a Cinderella's ugly sister-style trying on session.
If the glass slipper/shoe doesn't fit, bin it.

A PLACE FOR EVERYTHING

Essential in maintaining tidiness is the notion that everything should have a place to be stored and that an item should be returned to its allocated home when not in use. Today, find a home for any "floating" items throughout your house.

STORAGE HACK #5

Use ice cube trays to store
earrings in drawers.

CELEBRATE YOUR NEWLY TIDIED AREA

By this we don't mean throw it a party, rather decorate it. Maybe with a simple bunch of flowers, one treasured ornament, or a scented candle. A newly decluttered surface can seem rather inviting to place a little pile of papers or similar. If you decorate the area in this manner, you're reminding yourself that this is now an attractive, clear space — not a dumping ground.

CREATE
BEDTIME BLISS

Whatever your interior style — be it boho clutter, cosmopolitan chaos, or industrial chic — take a minimalist approach to your bedroom. You will be amazed at how creating a serene, uncluttered bedroom can really help your sleeping patterns. Create crisp, clear lines in the bedroom and your mind will follow.

"Get clear on what matters by getting rid of everything that doesn't."

– COURTNEY CARVER

"The most important work you will ever do will be within the walls of your own home."

– PRESIDENT HAROLD B. LEE

DEVISE A CLEANING SCHEDULE

Today, sit down and devise a cleaning schedule. Set aside some time each and every week to clean and tidy. If you stick to a strict schedule, you will stay on top of any approaching mess.

"The more you
have, the more
you dust!"

– UNKNOWN

"If you want to make an easy job seem mighty hard, just keep putting off doing it."

– OLIN MILLER

STORAGE HACK #6

Install a curtain rod in the cabinet under your sink and hang spray cleaning products from it.

WASH THE DISHES

…or put them straight in the dishwasher after using them. There's nothing like dirty dishes piled in the sink to make a room look instantly messy.

STORAGE HACK #7

Mount attractive doorknobs on the walls near your front door to create extra storage for coats, hats, and handbags.

"Life has a way
of setting things
in order and
leaving them be.
Very tidy, is life."

– JEAN ANOUILH

DELEGATE

If you're overwhelmed by the tidying task that lies ahead of you, call on others to help. If you live with other family members or friends, delegate some of the decluttering duties to them. Even the very youngest members of the household can be roped in to help with the tidying, and in turn you're helping them to develop good habits for life.

"Until we can manage time, we can manage nothing else."

– PETER DRUCKER

BUY MULTITASKING BEAUTY PRODUCTS

Shampoo AND conditioner? Not heard of the latest beauty buzz that is cleansing conditioner? Use a soap that also moisturizes, a cleansing wipe that also removes eye makeup, a blush that you can also use on your lips, a BB cream that performs the job of foundation and moisturizer — you get the idea. If you're mindful of what you're buying and the amount of space it's going to take up once you've got it home then it's actually pretty easy to cut the amount of cosmetics you need (and therefore your cosmetic clutter) in half.

"Our life is frittered away by detail. Simplify, simplify."

– HENRY DAVID THOREAU

STORAGE HACK #8

Use a wall-mounted spice rack to store nail polishes. A great way of being able to see what you've got and it makes for a colorful wall display.

STORAGE HACK #9

Use a hanging basket hung over the shower curtain rail to store bath toys or accessories.

"Effective tidying involves only two essential actions: discarding and deciding where to store things. Of the two, discarding must come first."

– MARIE KONDO

"Why the obsession with
worldly possessions?
When it's your time to go,
they have to stay behind,
so pack light."

– ALEX MORRITT

THE FOUR-BOX METHOD

As you set out to declutter an area, take four boxes along with you and label them: rubbish, give away, keep, or relocate. Each item in every room has to be placed into one of the four categories. No items can be ignored — this is a very thorough clearing technique.

AVOID TEMPTATION

If you know that you have a weakness for clothes, stay away from clothes shops or shopping online. Don't go to garage sales and antiques shops if you will be tempted to bring home things that will only clutter up your space again.

"Stuff has gotten a lot cheaper, but our attitudes towards it haven't changed correspondingly — we overvalue stuff."

– PAUL GRAHAM

"Clutter is symptomatic of delayed decision making."

– CYNTHIA KYRIAZIS

OPEN YOUR MAIL

It's so easy when rushing out of the door to just shove the mail in a pile to be dealt with at some unspecified later date. However, piles of unopened mail can build up alarmingly quickly. Make it a rule that you open your mail on the day it has been delivered and deal with it accordingly. It will usually fall into one of three categories: important but no action required, so file it; important and action is required (e.g. a bill to be paid), so do it; rubbish, so bin it. Simple!

STICK TO ROUTINES

Do things the same way every time: put your bag in one place as
you walk in the door, same for your keys, wallet, and umbrella.
When you need them, there they'll be.

"I knew then that the fewer items I was acquiring, dusting, packing, moving, and lugging around in life would free up my energy and time to create."

– DOROTHY BREININGER

"How many things
are there which
I do not want."

– SOCRATES

CHANGE YOUR PERSPECTIVE

It's amazing how much clutter we lose sight of in our houses because we have become so used to it being there. For a new perspective, invite a friend round to help you identify areas you need to clear out. Somebody who doesn't live in your house will be a far better editor of your stuff than you.

"You will never
be completely
ready. Start from
wherever you are."

– C.J. HAYDEN

FREECYCLE

A great way to get rid of old things is to sell or donate them. This is good for items that no longer work, as there are plenty of handy people out there who like to have a good go at mending things.

"When you live surrounded by clutter, it is impossible to have clarity about what you are doing in your life."

– KAREN KINGSTON

DIRT PREVENTION

Consider using rugs or mats at the entrances to all of your rooms to catch dirt and grit that can build up on floors and carpets.

DITCH OLD CLOTHES

Clothes are one of the biggest clutter culprits of any household. How many of us hold on to items of clothing we last wore circa 1998 because they evoke happy memories, disregarding the fact that we will never again be young enough/thin enough/in the right place to ever wear them? Chances are if you haven't worn something for over a year, you never will again.

"The first step in crafting the life you want is to get rid of everything you don't."

– JOSHUA BECKER

OUTDOOR SHELVING

Don't neglect your outside spaces when it comes to organizing and decluttering your home. Set up an outdoor shelf stocked with labelled buckets to store the things you use in your garden.

SCHEDULE 10-MINUTE TIDY-UPS

Regularly schedule in 10-minute tidy-ups for yourself and everyone else in your home. Make it a game for the whole family then follow it up with something relaxing and fun.

STORAGE HACK #10

Install a pegboard by the front door
to organize everyone's shoes.

COMPLETE EACH TASK
— COMPLETELY

Once you have decided where something needs to go, take it there. Now! Never keep bags for charity or boxes for friends in your house to deliver later. Take the bags and boxes out to the garbage or recycling immediately. If you're donating something or gifting it to a friend or family member, put the items in your car or make arrangements for dropping them off. Complete the task in its entirety.

"Eventually, time takes care of everything. The trouble with procrastination is that people give up on it too soon."

– ROBERT BRAULT

PAPERWORK

You need to have a good filing system in place at home. Use different colored folders or dividers to categorize paperwork however you wish to — for example, bills, invitations, and forms. It could also be useful to have a file each for different members of the household to store medical history, birth certificates, etc. Whatever system you put in place, it's essential to discard paperwork when you no longer need it, so carry out a regular sweep of the files so you don't keep short-term papers longer than is necessary.

STORAGE HACK #11

Attach envelopes to the inside of your notebooks to stash receipts and important documents that you need to keep close to hand.

"Every duty
which is bidden to
wait returns with
seven fresh duties
at its back."

– CHARLES KINGSLEY

HAVE A SYSTEM FOR SHOES

One that prevents you and/or your family from kicking them off as soon as you get in. Keep handy boxes or baskets near the door ready for shoes and boots. Tidying away shoes and boots immediately will prevent the floor from getting cluttered.

DECLUTTER ONE ITEM AT A TIME

Today, remove one unnecessary item from your house.
Do this each and every day.

"Joy is not in things; it is in us."

– RICHARD WAGNER

"The more you have, the more you are occupied. The less you have, the more free you are."

– MOTHER TERESA

TAKE A NOTE OF WHERE YOU'VE PUT THINGS

When you store away winter garments as spring approaches, be sure to note down where you've put everything. In your tidying frenzy you may end up with several boxes of storage. Be sure to label them. Go one step further and draw a plan of your house indicating where everything is stored.

CREATE WHITE SPACE

Choose one cluttered surface — a wall or a shelf, for example.
Clear absolutely everything from that surface and wipe it
clean. Leave it entirely empty for a week and then place one
— and only one — item on the wall or shelf. The rule is that
the item must be either beautiful or mean something to you.
Now step back and appreciate how much the white space
accentuates that one special item.

"When everything is precious, nothing is precious."

– ANDREW MELLEN

UNCLUTTERED GIFTS

Give and request gifts that won't cause clutter. For example, a trip out, movie passes, babysitting, chocolate, or wine.

USE CHALKBOARD PAINT

Paint one of your walls, or the side of a fridge or cabinet, with chalkboard paint. You can then use it to write recipes, shopping lists, meal planners or any other notes. This is a fantastic way to cut down on your paper clutter.

"If you can organize your kitchen, you can organize your life."

– LOUIS PARRISH

KITCHEN STORAGE RULES

When it comes to organizing your kitchen, keep the things you use most often at eye level, store heavy items below waist level and infrequently used items on high shelves.

"Later is the best friend of clutter."

— PETER WALSH

PERFORM A CLUTTER BUST

This is a great way to kick-start your journey toward a less cluttered environment and is a particularly good method for those who tend to deliberate over items. Choose a room and grab an empty laundry basket. Now, moving quickly, pick up each and every item that either doesn't belong in that room or is out of place and put it in the basket. Now empty it out onto the dining room table or a clear space on the floor and sort it into piles according to where they belong, including one for donations. Work through one pile at a time, putting everything back where it belongs.

"Keeping baggage from the past will leave no room for the happiness in the future."

– WAYNE L. MISNER

ROME WASN'T BUILT IN A DAY

Don't fall into the trap of thinking that once you have organized your space, you are done. You'll feel like a failure when you have to clean it up again in a month. Recognize that regular upkeep is a necessity, regardless of how clear and organized the space is now. Just enjoy how much easier the job is now you have a system.

"Good organizing
is not about
changing your
personality –
just your habits."

– UNKNOWN

SAVE BOOK COVERS

If you hold onto books because you have loved them but are unlikely to ever actually read them again, why not just save the covers? They serve the same purpose of evoking memory and appreciation only they take up a lot less space. You could even turn the covers into an artwork to display on your wall.

CATEGORIZE YOUR SHOES

There may not be much call for 10-inch sparkly stilettos on the school run, but we may like to think that one day we'll once again go to the ball. So, if you can't bring yourself to ditch all your spangly shoes, store one or two pairs as special occasion items. The key is to keep these separate from your everyday shoes.

STORAGE HACK #12

A paper towel holder turned on its side and mounted to the garage wall can make a great holder for string and thin wire.

"Tidiness...makes life easier and more agreeable, does harm to no one and actually saves time and trouble to the person who practices it: there must be an ominous flaw to explain why millions of generations continue to reject it."

– FREYA STARK

START AN EXIT DRAWER

This could be a drawer in your hallway, a basket in a cupboard, a tote bag hung on the back of the front door. This is the place for everything that needs to leave the house when you do — letters to post, bills to pay or borrowed items to return to friends or neighbors. The method is simple: look in that drawer or bag every time you leave the house. This will help you to keep the house clear of things that don't need to be there.

"Have a time and place for everything, and do everything in its time and place, and you will not only accomplish more, but have far more leisure than those who are always hurrying."

– TRYON EDWARDS

CONSIDER OFF-SITE STORAGE

If you have belongings that you really need to hang on to but don't have room for them, renting a self-storage unit can help get rid of clutter around your home.

"When we clear the physical clutter from our lives, we literally make way for inspiration and 'good, orderly direction' to enter."

– JULIA CAMERON

"Your most treasured moments are not in the attic."

‒ COURTNEY CARVER

FOLD YOUR CLOTHES SO THEY STAND UP

This one is a tip from the tidiness guru herself, Marie Kondo. Instead of folding your clothes and laying them flat on top of each other, fold them and store them standing up. This way, you can instantly find what you're looking for, and you don't make a mess trying to pull something out from the bottom of the pile.

"Don't agonize. Organize."

– FLORYNCE KENNEDY

"Life is too complicated not to be orderly."

– MARTHA STEWART

STORAGE HACK #13

Use Velcro to store remote controls on the inside of cupboard doors or the side of a shelving unit. Attach one part to the remote control, and the other wherever you want to keep it.

The National Association of Professional Organizers reports we spend one year of our lives looking for lost items.

FENG SHUI YOUR HOME

Make bringing in elements of Feng Shui into your home part of your spring clean. The element associated with spring is wood, which governs our enthusiasm for living, growing, expanding, and taking action for our desires and dreams. Bring more wood into your home with potted plants: place one near the front door, one near the living room and one in the bedroom. Consider adding some wooden décor such as a wooden vase.

"There are tons of things in your home and life that you don't use, need, or even particularly want. They just came into your life as impulsive flotsam and jetsam and never found a good exit. Whether you're aware of it or not, this clutter creates indecision and distractions."

– TIM FERRISS

ENCOURAGE TIDINESS IN CHILDREN

Teach young children to put toys and games away before they get out the next thing they want to play with. For example, if your child wants a toy on a high shelf but hasn't put away a game from earlier, gently let them know that they cannot play with the new toy until they have tidied up the old one.

Research has found that the average 10-year-old in Britain owns 238 toys but plays with just 12 daily.

SIMPLIFY YOUR SURROUNDINGS

Is there really a need for several boxes of tea, packs of cookies and jars of coffee to be stored on your kitchen worktop? Choose your favorite one and keep it handy; store the others in a cabinet as close to your kettle as possible.

"Less is more."

– LUDWIG MIES VAN DER ROHE

PEN PURGE

Many of us have houses full of pens, yet when it comes to finding one when we need it, they're never to be seen. Today, have a pen purge and bin all the pens that have dried up because you've left the lids off, or have leaked all over the interior of your bag or pocket, and invest in one beautiful pen that has its designated home.

"Get rid of things
or you'll spend
your whole life
tidying up."

— MARGUERITE DURAS

VIRTUAL TIDYING

Decluttering and tidying should not just be confined to the physical world. A cluttered online life can cause just as much stress as an untidy physical environment. So today, make the effort to clear your inbox of clutter by unsubscribing from everything that no longer serves a valid purpose in your life.

"You don't have to be perfect to be organized."

– MONIKA KRISTOFFERSON

NO TIME IS
NO EXCUSE

Stop telling yourself that you don't have the time to organize
your home and declutter. However much time it takes, you will
get it back and then some. No more searching through piles of
stuff for what you need; no more getting distracted by the clutter
surrounding you. And once you have established good tidiness
and cleaning habits it will take just a fraction of the time to
maintain your house.

"You will never find time for anything. If you want time you must make it."

— CHARLES BUXTON

"It always seems impossible until it's done."

— NELSON MANDELA

TRY THE COAT HANGER EXPERIMENT

Having trouble deciding which clothes you can do without? To identify wardrobe pieces to clear out, hang all your clothes with the hangers in the reverse direction. After you wear an item, return it to the wardrobe with the hanger facing the correct direction. After six months, you'll have a clear picture of which clothes you can easily discard.

TAKE A PICTURE

If you find that you're being oversentimental in your efforts to declutter, take a picture of the sentimental object you're having trouble letting go of and keep that instead. It's likely to take up far less room and will serve as a reminder of that special item.

"Treasure your relationships, not your possessions."

– ANTHONY J. D'ANGELO

DITCH THE FAD ITEMS

Toasted sandwich maker anyone? Banana slicer? If you haven't used it in over two years, chances are you don't need it, so ditch it.

"Clutter is one of the greatest enemies of efficiency and stealers of time."

– DON ASLETT

CLEAR OUT THE KITCHEN CABINETS

How many plates, bowls, and glasses do you really need? Perhaps you wish you entertained more so you're keeping stores of crockery "just in case." Review your life and how you really live it, not how you aspire to live it. If you do this with honesty, it's amazing how much you will realize you don't actually need.

STORAGE HACK #14

Use a small flowerpot with a drip
tray to store sponges, scrubbers,
and other dishwashing supplies
by the sink.

FOOD CULL

Throw out any food that has gone past its expiry date, including those dried herbs you've had for years that taste like dust and any jars and bottles that have been opened for too long.

ROTATE THE FOOD IN YOUR KITCHEN CABINETS

When you come to put new groceries away, store them at the back, bringing older items to the front so you don't lose track of what you have and end up hoarding old items for months, even years.

"Cleanliness and order are not matters of instinct; they are matters of education, and like most great things, you must cultivate a taste for them."

– BENJAMIN DISRAELI

STORE KITCHEN ESSENTIALS IN GLASS-FRONTED CABINETS

Glass-fronted cabinets will be a great incentive for you to keep your crockery and glasses organized and tidy.

STORAGE HACK #15

Use stacked bamboo steamers for kitchen storage. These are a perfect place to keep vegetables like onions and garlic because they offer plenty of ventilation for continued freshness.

CLEAN YOUR WINDOWSILLS

Often forgotten in regular cleaning routines, but window ledges are places where damp and mildew can build up, so focus on these today. Remove anything stored on them and enjoy the extra light pouring through the windows!

"One always has time enough, if one will apply it well."

– GOETHE

PLAY CARDS

Write household tasks on index cards and draw one each day. This becomes your chore for the day. This is also a great way to get the kids involved — make a special box for them containing child-friendly chores so they can work alongside you on their own job of the day.

"It does not require money to be neat, clean and dignified."

– GANDHI

"It is preoccupation with possession, more than anything else, that prevents men from living freely and nobly."

– BERTRAND RUSSELL

STORAGE HACK #16

Use a wine rack as a towel holder.
Roll the towels and slot them into
the holes designed for bottles.

"Clear your stuff.
Clear your mind."

– ERIC M. RIDDLE

CLOTHES CONTROL

Always immediately hang clothing you take off when you walk in the door. If you need to wash it, put it straight in your laundry basket. Don't just throw it on the bed or a chair. Once that starts, it's all too easy for more mess to follow.

"Give me the discipline to get rid of the stuff that's not important, the freedom to savor the stuff that gives me joy, and the patience not to worry about the stuff that's messy but not hurting anybody."

– VINITA HAMPTON WRIGHT

SELL, SELL, SELL

Gather all of your unwanted items and sell them online.
Treat yourself to something like a dinner out with the proceeds.
It's a great incentive to do it again.

"In the end, the treasure of life is missed by those who hold on and gained by those who let go."

– LAO TZU

SHOP WITH PURPOSE AND A LIST

Focused shopping will help you avoid careless purchasing and reduce your clutter. Set out on targetted shopping trips and only buy items on your list.

"Tis better to donate than to accumulate."

– JOSHUA BECKER

"Trying to be happy by accumulating possessions is like trying to satisfy hunger by taping sandwiches all over your body."

– GEORGE CARLIN

DIVIDE AND CONQUER

An essential component in bringing order to your drawers is to use plastic or wooden drawer dividers, or make your own from covered cereal boxes. You must be able to compartmentalize so you can see exactly what's in each drawer and reach it easily.

STORAGE HACK #17

Use empty bottles
as bracelet holders.

FREE UP YOUR SHELF SPACE

Ditch the DVD and Blu-Ray boxes and store the disks in plastic sleeves in small baskets, arranged alphabetically.

"What you do today
can improve all
your tomorrows."

– RALPH MARSTON

STORE KITCHEN APPLIANCES OUT OF SIGHT

Toasters, coffee makers, kettles — they all take up space. And while it may not seem like much, the first time you prepare dinner on a counter without them present, you'll really notice the difference. If you think it's going to be a hassle putting them away every morning, don't. It takes less than ten seconds to put each appliance away.

STORAGE HACK #18

Sort out your food containers by
using wire CD racks in your cabinet
to store your plastic lids.

ONE IN, ONE OUT

Make like a nightclub bouncer and adopt a one-in, one-out rule. When you buy a new item, something else that you already own must be discarded or donated. This is a simple way to keep the numbers down.

In a recent study by IKEA, 31% of those surveyed reported more satisfaction from clearing out their closet than they did after sex.

CREATE A CAPSULE WARDROBE

Too many clothes yet nothing to wear? Then it's time to pare down your wardrobe. Try to streamline it so it contains just 20 core items. A woman's capsule collection might look something like this:

1 dress, 2 jackets, 3 skirts, 3 jumpers, 2 trousers, 2 jeans, 3 coats, 1 shirt, 3 t-shirts or casual tops

Of course, it can be adapted to suit your tastes and lifestyle, but by creating a minimal wardrobe you're eliminating small yet draining decisions that you have to make every morning of your life.

STORAGE HACK #19

Utilize the floor space in your wardrobe by installing shelves or cubbyholes at the base and you'll never have to rifle through items strewn across the floor.

"Happiness is
not found in things
you possess,
but in what you
have the courage
to release."

– NATHANIEL HAWTHORNE

USE CLEAR STORAGE CONTAINERS

Store toys in clear containers so children can see what's in them and you can sort them before the contents get out of hand.

"Good order is the foundation of all things."

– EDMUND BURKE

TAKE THE 12–12–12 CHALLENGE

A simple task of locating 12 items to throw away, 12 items to donate, and 12 items to be returned to their proper home can be a fun way to quickly organize 36 things in your house. Get the whole household involved and even turn it into a competition.

"Everything you own, owns you."

– WAYNE DYER

ROTATE YOUR RUGS

If you have rugs in your home, rotate them to avoid wear and tear (of those in high footfall areas) and fading (of any that catch the sunlight).

"What is not started today is never finished tomorrow."

– GOETHE

"Possessions are usually diminished by possession."

– NIETZSCHE

CHORES WHILE ON THE PHONE

Why not multitask and do some chores during a long phone conversation? Some of us can manage to chat on the phone for an hour at a time and meanwhile nothing is getting done. Why not do a bit of dusting or fold the laundry while on the phone? It's a great way to take the stress out of chores as you barely notice you're doing them while chatting away!

"Time is a created thing. To say 'I don't have time' is to say 'I don't want to.'"

– LAO TZU

"Beginnings are always messy."

JOHN GALSWORTHY

ESTABLISH CLUTTER PRESERVES

Even the tidiest among us still throw their clothes on the floor from time to time, or shove things in a random drawer just to get them out of sight. Accept reality by establishing dedicated clutter preserves. In these, clutter may live freely, as long as it stays within boundaries. In a bedroom, for example, a chair could become the clutter preserve. Clothing may be thrown with abandon, so long as it's thrown only on the chair.

"Clearing the clutter in your physical space will go a long way toward clearing the clutter in your mind and your relationships."

– PETER WALSH

USE YOUR WALLS

If you don't have a lot of floor space, then make use of your wall space. Put up more shelves or bookcases to help organize your belongings. Store upwards not outwards!

"Art has something to do with the achievement of stillness in the midst of chaos."

– SAUL BELLOW

ADOPT THE
80/20 RULE

We tend to only wear 20% of the clothes we own 80% of the time. This rule is true of other things as well, such as books, DVDs, toys and more. Your mission is to get rid of the things you don't use 80% of the time.

"Be a ruthless editor
of what you allow
into your home.
Ask yourselves
'what does this object
mean to me?'"

– NATE BERKUS

NEVER GO UPSTAIRS OR DOWNSTAIRS EMPTY-HANDED

Keep a small basket at the top of the stairs and another at the bottom. Items that need to be returned to rooms upstairs get put in the basket at the bottom, while those that need to be returned to rooms downstairs go into the basket at the top.

"You're the boss of clutter, not the other way around."

– MONIKA KRISTOFFERSON

"If you have clutter in your real life, your tangible life, then it really adds to the emotional clutter in your mind."

— GIULIANA RANCIC

ORGANIZE YOUR BILLS

After you've paid your bills, the easiest way to keep track of them is to arrange them, by month, in an accordion file. Each year replace the file and go through month by month to see what to scan or keep.

DONATE

Make today a day that you donate unwanted items and benefit not only from a tidier home, but the feel-good factor that charitable giving brings.

"Have nothing in your house that you do not know to be useful or believe to be beautiful."

– WILLIAM MORRIS

GET A HANDHELD LABEL MAKER

You can get as many containers, boxes, and baskets as you like, but they are useless if you can't easily tell what is inside. Label them swiftly and neatly with a handheld label maker to solve the issue.

HAVE A CAR BOOT OR GARAGE SALE

This is a great way to see how your clutter could become someone else's treasure. Seeing people delighted with your unwanted items will inspire you to get rid of more.

"Clear your stuff.
Clear your mind."

– ERIC M. RIDDLE

CATEGORIZE YOUR WARDROBE

Sort your clothes in categories — work, casual, sports — and enjoy how much easier and quicker it is to find and select your clothes.

"Organize your life around your dreams, and watch them come true."

– UNKNOWN

CHARITY BOX

Consider keeping a box or basket in the bottom of your wardrobe to use for thrift store donations. That way you can pop unwanted items straight in the box, preventing any procrastination and delaying tactics.

"When you have Enough, you have everything you need. There's nothing extra to weigh you down, distract, or distress you. Enough is a fearless place. A trusting place. An honest and self-observant place ... To let go of clutter, then, is not deprivation; it's lightening up and opening up space and time for something new and wonderful to happen."

– VICKI ROBIN

HAVE A CLEARING OUT PARTY

Arrange for a group of friends to come and help you clear out your clutter. To give them an incentive, other than supplying wine, tell them they can take any clothes or ornaments that you've decided you can live without.

"Clutter-clearing is modern-day alchemy."

– DENISE LINN

USE YOUR IMAGINATION

As you sort through your belongings, try asking yourself questions such as "If I saw this in a store now would I buy it?" By imagining yourself in a different scenario you are distancing yourself from the item and will hopefully be able to form a more objective opinion about it.

"Look at your own life. Has it become overly complex? Have you found yourself burdened by too many possessions or responsibilities? Take a deep breath and ask yourself: 'What steps can I take to reduce the clutter so that I may live simply and joyously?'"

– DOUGLAS BLOCH

EDIT, CONSTANTLY

As good as our simplifying intentions may be, it is almost inevitable that we accumulate more stuff. Throughout the year, try to evaluate areas as you use them, assessing whether you really need all that you can see.

"If it doesn't make you feel fabulous: don't do it, don't buy it, don't keep it."

– LIZ K ZOOK

STORAGE HACK #20

Install a shelf over the top of your bathroom door. You'll be surprised by how much you can fit here even if you have very little space between your door and the ceiling.

MAKE OVER YOUR BATHROOM CABINET

Once you've cleared out your bathroom cabinet, give it a makeover with an assorted collection of vintage cups and glassware. These can hold toiletries such as cotton balls, toothbrushes, and toothpaste.

STORAGE HACK #21

Install a magazine holder inside a bathroom cabinet door if you have the space. It's the perfect size and shape to hold a hairdryer stored upside-down.

"It takes as much energy to wish as it does to plan."

– ELEANOR ROOSEVELT

GET A
COLOR SCHEME

If you don't already have a color scheme in your bedroom,
it probably looks more cluttered than it actually is.
Just choosing a few key colors and coordinating them
with your décor creates a tidier feel.

"Out of clutter, find simplicity. From discord, find harmony. In the middle of difficulty lies opportunity."

– ALBERT EINSTEIN

STORAGE HACK #22

Use magnets to give yourself some
extra storage space in the kitchen.
Items such as metallic spice jars and
utensils can both stick to magnets.
You can then use the magnets
to stick them to the side of your
fridge, or beneath kitchen cabinets
if you fix magnetic strips there.

THAT DRAWER

Elastic bands, dried up pens, balls of Blu-tack, old batteries —
somehow they have all found their way in there. Today, tackle
this drawer. Once you've binned the rubbish. if there isn't an
obvious place for the rest of the contents, don't be afraid to keep
a "miscellaneous" drawer — but make sure you categorize and
sort the contents into clear boxes.

"Simplicity is realizing what you need rather than what you want."

– APOORVE DUBEY

BE SELECTIVE
WITH ORNAMENTS

More often than not, ornaments are nothing more than dust collectors. Today, gather all of your ornaments and put them together in one place. Are they beautiful? Do they make you happy or ignite happy memories? If not, bin them.

"Clutter is a weight that has built on top of you so gradually, you don't even realize anymore that it is holding you down."

– MARY JOHANSON

PURGE YOUR KITCHEN CONTAINERS

If the lid to a container is long lost, get rid of the base. If you need to buy more to replace them, select square boxes as they take up less room and are easier to stack.

"Clutter is stuck energy. The word 'clutter' derives from the Middle English word 'clotter,' which means to coagulate – and that's about as stuck as you can get."

– KAREN KINGSTON

MAKE A BINDER FOR KEEPSAKES

Store special birthday cards, letters, pictures and similar items properly in binders with clear page protectors so you can see what you have. This will serve the double purpose of keeping your treasures safe while making you more selective with what you keep.

"Make space in your life for what matters."

– UNKNOWN

HANDBAG OVERHAUL

Your handbag needs an organized system, just as your home does. Group similar items together and place them in individual pouches or purses within your bag. Keys and travel cards that need to be accessed quickly and easily belong in an outer zipped area. Edit on a weekly basis to make sure you're carrying only essential items around with you.

"It's all about finding the calm in the chaos."

– DONNA KARAN

EARN MONEY FOR ELECTRICAL ITEMS

The rate of technology advances means we're often left with out-of-date electrical goods. If you have an old phone or tablet lying around, look for companies that will exchange old handsets and electrical goods for money and really cash in on your clear-outs.

"Begin while others are procrastinating. Work while others are wishing."

– WILLIAM ARTHUR WARD

MAKE LINEN DUST SHADES

A tip from Martha Stewart to protect books from dust is to hang crisp lengths of linen from shelves. These shades should cover the top portion of the shelves only (where dust creeps in), leaving the book spines on view.

According to The National Soap & Detergent Association in the US, getting rid of clutter will reduce housework by 40 percent.

RETUNE YOUR MIND

If it makes you anxious to give away things that you might one day need, remind yourself that you are not really giving them away. Instead, you're trading them in for something far better — an uncluttered home where you feel at peace.

"We are not rich by what we possess but by what we can do without."

– IMMANUEL KANT

SIMPLIFY
YOUR STORAGE

Expensive or complicated storage equipment is
often unnecessary. Sometimes something as simple
as a shoebox does a great job.

"Early in my career I felt that organization would destroy my creativity. Whereas now, I feel the opposite. Discipline is the concrete that allows you to be creative."

– VERNA GIBSON

REMEMBER YOU ARE THE MOST IMPORTANT GUEST IN YOUR HOME

Don't fall into the habit of living in mess and having tidying spurts just before people are due to come round. Clear up for yourself, not for visitors, so that you have a lovely, bright space in which to live. Paint the walls a color that makes you smile, surround yourself only with things that make you happy, buy yourself flowers to arrange throughout the house — do it for yourself, not to create a show home for the benefit of guests.

"I am thankful for a lawn that needs mowing, windows that need cleaning and gutters that need fixing because it means I have a home... I am thankful for the piles of laundry and ironing because it means my loved ones are nearby."

– NANCIE J. CARMODY

READ AND RECYCLE

There is no need to keep magazines and other reading material (apart from books) once you have read them. If there's an article or recipe you'd like to keep, tear it out and keep it in a binder designated for that purpose. Repeat the mantra: read and recycle.

"Today is the day to let go of things that no longer serve you."

- KATRINA MAYER

DECLUTTER YOUR TV BOX

Delete all the programs you have stored that you won't want to watch again, won't have time to watch or don't need to watch.

FREE UP FLOOR SPACE

Hanging storage is a great way to clear floor space. Particularly
good for children's soft toys in the bedroom (create a hammock
for them). Or if you're tight on kitchen space, suspend your pots
and pans from ceiling racks.

STORAGE HACK #23

Consider buying a hanging shoe rack for your closet door. This is a great way to utilize otherwise wasted space and you can use the pockets for more than just shoes. They are great for consolidating hairpins, jewelry, and makeup, freeing up space on your dressing table and in your drawers.

STORE OUT-OF-SEASON ITEMS

These items can take up precious space unnecessarily. Seasonal clothing, blankets, and accessories can all be stored away off-season. That means things like scarves, gloves, and coats during the summer, and light summery clothing and lighter duvets during the colder months.

"The secret to successful decluttering is this: you will never get organized if you don't have a vision for the life you want."

– PETER WALSH

MAKE BEING TIDY EASY

Don't hide your laundry basket in the back of a closet. Instead, use an open basket that you can throw your clothes into from across the room. Choose open containers for things you use often, like toiletries and cooking supplies, to make it easier to get to them and put them away. Don't use boxes with lids stacked on top of one another for items that you need to access daily.

"You don't need
more space.
You need
less stuff."

– JOSHUA BECKER

STORAGE HACK #24

Transform a simple cube organizer into a stylish storage space for glassware, attractive crockery, table linens, and other entertaining accessories.

"The best time for planning a book is while you're doing the dishes."

– AGATHA CHRISTIE

KITCHEN CLEANLINESS

Never let the sun set on an argument – or a dirty kitchen. Even if you can't get to the dishes right after a meal, make sure the kitchen is clean before bedtime to prevent an unmanageable mess that you'll have to face in the morning.

"If you spend too much time thinking about a thing, you'll never get it done."

– BRUCE LEE

FORM GOOD HABITS

The more you do it, the more you'll do it! When you have decluttered and organized your house and witnessed the results, you'll feel motivated to keep going. Once you get into the swing of a new tidying regime, it will soon become habit.

According to a study conducted
by a Boston marketing firm,
the average person will burn
55 minutes a day looking for things.

STORAGE HACK #25

Place your rolls of wrapping
paper upright in a garment bag
to be hung in a closet.

ORGANIZE YOUR WIRES

If you have lots of screens, consoles and other technology, take the time to bundle your cords together and tape them out of the way. Label your wires with tags and you will find them much easier to manage.

"It is easier to be happy when you are not surrounded by the confusion and the clutter of life."

– UNKNOWN

MAKE A LIST

Many professional organizers recommend that you write a list of areas in your home to declutter and then begin with the easiest. When you've decluttered one area, stop. By working down your list tackling only one area at a time, you can easily fit it into any schedule.

"The journey of a thousand miles begins with one step."

– LAO TZU

BUY LESS STUFF

Of course one way to keep things tidier is to avoid clutter in the first place. It's quite simple — buy less stuff. Try the 30-day rule: If you're in a store and feel the need to purchase a non-essential item, take a note of what the item is, with the price and date alongside, then leave the store. Wait for 30 days. During that month think about the item and how much you really need it, what it would bring to your life. If after the 30 days you still want to buy it, then do. More often than not the urge to splurge will have left you during this waiting time.

"The greatest wealth is to live content with little."

— PLATO

"Collect moments not things."

– UNKNOWN

USE APPS

Make Post-It notes a thing of the past by going digital.
Whether it's a web link, a screenshot, a photo, or a note to
self, use an app such as Evernote to store it all in one place
and cut down on your paper clutter.

ORGANIZE YOUR BEDDING

Keep your linen closet super tidy by organizing bedding into sets. Place matching sheets, pillowcases, and duvet covers inside one of the pillowcases from the set, so when it's time to change the bed everything you need is together in one place.

"The man who removes a mountain begins by carrying away small stones."

– CONFUCIUS

GROUP LIKE WITH LIKE

Designate areas for different types of items; for example, stationery, crafts, important documents, invitations, wires and cords, batteries, plugs, and gadgets. This way you'll know exactly where to look for something when you need it.

STORAGE HACK #26

Architectural plaster moldings make brilliant rails for storing your best heels. Paint the moldings a bright color and fix to the wall in neat rows to create an eye-catching wall display.

BUY FURNITURE THAT FEATURES STORAGE SPACE

When buying furniture, consider your storage needs at the same time. Some beds, tables and other types of furniture offer drawers and other nooks where you can stash belongings to immediately eliminate clutter.

STORAGE HACK #27

If you don't have a coffee table, why not put wheels on a picnic basket for instant added storage with rustic charm?

PHOTOGRAPHS

If you're a traditionalist clinging on to the predigital era, chances are you'll have piles of photographs somewhere in the house. Sort through these and if they're good enough to keep, frame them or create a collage and put them on the wall to free up precious cupboard and drawer space.

"Keep only those
things that speak
to your heart."

– MARIE KONDO

PURGE ON A REGULAR BASIS

If you go too long without clear outs you will find yourself overwhelmed by too much stuff and be tempted not to deal with it. Develop a habit of sorting through your things and getting rid of items you no longer want or need.

"Use decluttering or purging as a meditation. Each item is part of your story. Thank the item for its story, close that chapter and move on."

– JENNIFER PHELPS

SLEEK STORAGE

Floating shelves are great for small rooms since they don't take up nearly as much space as bulky, standalone storage units. Or consider framing a door with shelves as this is space that tends to be under-utilized.

DEVELOP A LAUNDRY HABIT

Do one load of laundry every day.
You will never have a mounting pile of dirty washing
if you get into the habit of doing this.

"In plain words, chaos was the law of nature, order was the dream of man."

– HENRY BROOKE ADAMS

KNOW WHAT YOU LIKE AND STICK TO IT

Choose your products wisely and stick to them. You don't need a dozen different bottles of lotions and potions when two good ones will do the job perfectly well. This philosophy can be applied to anything from cosmetics to cleaning products.

"Buy less, choose well."

– VIVIENNE WESTWOOD

ORGANIZE YOUR MAIL

Have a system for incoming and outgoing mail, such as letter trays, baskets, or standing racks in your entryway.

"Never do tomorrow what you can do today, procrastination is the thief of time."

– UNKNOWN

One in three UK households
contains enough junk to fill
a small bedroom.

LISTEN TO MUSIC WHILE YOU TIDY

It's surprisingly easy to make tidying and organizing fun by putting together a playlist and listening to music while you clean.

"The world hijacks our passion and directs it toward material things. But nobody gets to the end of their life wishing they had bought more junk."

– JOSHUA BECKER

AVOID DISTRACTIONS

To stay focused on the job at hand place an exit box in the doorway of the room you're decluttering. When you find a misplaced item — for example, a mug while cleaning the living room — place it in the box rather than strolling to the kitchen and ending up sidetracked. Return the items to their rightful place only once you've finished decluttering the room.

"If you want a thing done well, do it yourself."

– NAPOLEON BONAPARTE

LIVE WITH LESS

Experiment with numbers. For example, Courtney Carver invented Project 333 to challenge people to wear only 33 articles of clothing for 3 months. Adjust the rules as you need by picking your own numbers. The important thing is to challenge yourself to live with less.

"A human being has a natural desire to have more of a good thing than he needs."

– MARK TWAIN

HAVE AN ANNUAL KITCHEN CULL

Every year, take an inventory of all utensils, cookware, and crockery. Get rid of unnecessary duplicates, items that are damaged beyond repair, or things you no longer use.

"Letting go gives us freedom, and freedom is the only condition for happiness."

– THICH NHAT HANH

FIVE QUESTIONS TO ASK YOURSELF BEFORE YOU BUY

Before you buy anything new (and potentially bring more clutter into your home) ask yourself the following questions:

1. Why am I buying this?

2. Do I love it?

3. Do I have space for it?

4. Do I already own something similar or the same?

5. How will purchasing this item make my life better or bring me joy?

"He who would travel happily must travel light."

– ANTOINE DE SAINT-EXUPÉRY

GET YOUR CHILDREN INTO GOOD DECLUTTERING HABITS

Ask them to fill a box with toys they don't play with anymore and get them to accompany you to a thrift store or to see a friend with younger children who may make better use of them. As well as the practical result of having a tidier house, you're fostering a kind attitude of giving and sharing in your children.

STORAGE HACK #28

Keep coloring books, pads, and art supplies organized in a dish-drying rack. Stack the books like plates between the prongs. Store pens, crayons, and pencils in the utensil caddy.

DON'T BUY IN BULK

Another clutter avoidance technique is not to buy in bulk. Don't fall for the buy-one-get-one-free offers that supermarkets are so fond of. You'll end up with more than you have room to store, and quite possibly more than you'd ever be able to use before the best before dates anyway. It's often a false economy and a practice that gets you into bad hoarding habits.

STORAGE HACK #29

An old tissue box makes a great dispenser for plastic bags. Simply pull one out when you need one.

LOST AND FOUND

Set up a lost-and-found system in an area of your house. Assign each family member their own different colored basket. As you clean and come across their misplaced belongings put them in their basket. Make a rule that family members need to empty their baskets at the end of each day/every other day/once a week, depending on what works for you.

"Clutter in your physical surroundings will clutter your mind and spirit."

– KANEISHA GRAYSON

WAVE GOODBYE TO MULTIPLES

Multiple items that perform the same function have to go. Everyone has their own weakness in this category — whether it's another pair of almost identical black heels, phone charger leads, headphones, or moisturizers — the end result is the same: more unnecessary clutter.

"Instead of figuring out how to make ends meet, work on having fewer ends."

– UNKNOWN

UN-DECORATE

It's possible to have too much going on in your living areas, making it feel cluttered and overcrowded. Try cutting back on the number of cushions and hanging pictures. Add floating shelves to the walls to remove photographs or ornaments that may be crowding your tabletops.

"You only lose
what you cling to."

– BUDDHA

KEEP A "MAYBE" BOX

If you're a sentimental type prone to procrastination or an avid hoarder this method may suit you. Keep a "maybe" box where you can place all of the items you're not sure you can do without. Revisit the box in six months and throw out anything you haven't thought about once.

"You will find that it's necessary to let things go; simply for the reason that they are heavy."

– C. JOYBELL C.

GOOD ENOUGH IS ENOUGH

Your house will not look perfect and your closet won't look like something from a catalogue; you have a life to lead and real humans living in your house. You will ultimately be disappointed if perfection is your goal. The aim is to set up a space that works well for your needs, not to create a show home.

"Strive for progress
not for perfection."

– UNKNOWN

LET THE LIGHT IN

Clean your windows! It is truly surprising how much extra light a cleaned window lets in and the light brightens and freshens up everything in the home.

"In the kitchen and in life, clean up as you go."

– UNKNOWN

Studies have shown that working in an orderly environment promotes healthy choices and generosity.

CLUTTER CLEARING MANTRA

How long has it been since I used this?

Does it work?

Do I like it?

Do I have more? How many do I need?

If I keep this what can I get rid of to make room for it?

"Out of
clutter, find."

– UNKNOWN

RECYCLE JUNK MAIL IMMEDIATELY

Take note of the natural flow of mail into your home. Place a recycling container close to where you're usually tempted to pile up your post and catch most of that junk mail before it even reaches a surface in your home. The added bonus is that you're even less likely to read it, so you free yourself from one method of advertising bombardment.

"Free clutter is no different to any other kind of clutter — it gets in the way."

– KIRSTIE ALLSOPP

DIGITIZE

Paperwork piling up? Scan documents and store them
electronically to cut back on paper clutter.

"In the never-ending battle between order and chaos, clutter sides with chaos every time. Anything that you possess that does not add to your life or your happiness eventually becomes a burden."

– JOHN ROBBINS

"The sooner I fall behind, the more time I have to catch up."

– UNKNOWN

HANG CLEANING TOOLS

Use wall hooks to keep brooms and mops off the floor. These could be placed inside a closet door, on the walls of a utility room, or tucked away neatly behind a door.

"The question of what you want to own is actually the question of how you want to live your life."

– MARIE KONDO

There are 300,000 items in the average American home.

TURN IT INTO
A GAME

Tap into your family's/housemate's competitive nature and transform the task of tidying into a fun game. Time different members of the household to perform various decluttering and cleaning chores and award prizes to the winners.

On average, we spend 6 minutes looking for our keys in the morning.

FLOWERS, FLOWERS EVERYWHERE

Don't underestimate the value of fresh flowers. Place them in rooms around the house once you've tidied them. They provide a brilliant finishing touch and work wonders at distracting from anything that may not be perfectly tidy.

IDENTIFY CLUTTER HOTSPOTS

Place attractive baskets in places where clutter tends to pile up and put the items away before the baskets overflow.

ORGANIZE FIRST, BUY LATER

Don't go out and buy a load of storage supplies before you sort through your house. All of those attractive boxes and baskets are very enticing, but they won't be of any use unless they fit the space and hold exactly what you need them to hold. Until you've cleared out and know exactly what you need, hold off buying anything or you may well end up with the storage containers themselves cluttering up your home.

STORAGE HACK #30

Transfer board games into labelled plastic drawers to save space.

HIRE A DUMPSTER

If you have a lot to get rid of, consider hiring a dumpster. Going to the trouble and expense will give you great incentive to fill it, as well as a deadline.

"Get rid of clutter and you may find it was blocking the door you've been looking for."

– KATRINA MAYER

INDULGE IN THE ACT OF GIFTING

Give away one item each day. Re-gift your unwanted items to friends, neighbors, anyone in need. By this we mean the good stuff worth saving; don't just transfer your rubbish to another person's house. This is a great way to clear your house and has the added side effect of leaving you with a warm fuzzy feeling sparked by your generosity.

STORAGE HACK #31

Stack shelves within shelves: Place plastic-coated wire shelves in kitchen cabinets to double storage capacity for dishes, cups, glasses, and pans.

REORGANIZE

You don't always have to throw things away to declutter.
It could be that what you do have is just badly organized.
Don't be afraid to get things out of drawers and cupboards
in order to re-sort them — restack books on bookshelves and
refold your clothes. This may seem counterintuitive when
you're trying to tidy things away, but the extra space you'll
gain makes it well worth the effort.

"Clear up the clutter.
It diverts your attention,
hampers your thinking,
dilutes your efforts,
and hinders your progress."

– MERRILL DOUGLASS

SHELF APPEAL

Paint shelves in attractive eye-catching colors
or cover them with beautiful wallpaper and
you're less likely to cover them in clutter.

STORAGE HACK #32

Instead of having to locate your remote controls from their usual spot stuffed between the sofa cushions, why not put an attractive wide-mouthed vase on your side table or a shelf to store your remotes in?

END OF THE DAY SWEEP

Take anywhere between 5 to 15 minutes at the end of each day to perform an evening sweep. Go from room to room returning items to their homes and straightening. The key to this is to do it quickly and with purpose, and do it before you've sat down with that end-of-day drink.

CLEAN AS YOU GO

When making dinner or hosting a party, avoid a massive clean-up job by washing dishes, loading the dishwasher, and wiping the counters as you're preparing the food or undertaking other tasks.

VISUALIZE THE SPACE YOU WANT

It can be really helpful to stop and visualize what you want to achieve: the space you want to create and the kind of home you want to live in. This can really help to inspire you to start your tidying spree.

"Simplicity is an acquired taste. Mankind, left free, instinctively complicates life."

– KATHARINE FULLERTON GEROULD

SHRED OLD DOCUMENTS

Any papers containing personal information that you no longer need should be shredded to protect you from identity theft.

"Don't say you don't have enough time. You have exactly the same number of hours per day that were given to Helen Keller, Pasteur, Michelangelo, Mother Teresa, Leonardo Da Vinci, Thomas Jefferson, and Albert Einstein."

– H. JACKSON BROWN, JR

JEWELRY

Sort through your jewelry, unknot necklaces, throw away odd earrings (unless that's your style). A good way to store jewelry is to hang it from hooks on a decorative corkboard. This also helps you to be selective in what you're keeping — if you don't like it enough to have it hanging on display, it's unlikely you'll ever want to wear it.

DARE TO BE MINIMALIST

Too much furniture can make even large rooms look cluttered. Stick to the basics when it comes to furniture and your house will look tidier before you've even begun.

"Clutter is evidence of excess."

– CRISTIN FRANK

RECYCLE

Let these recycling options inspire you to have a clear out:

Toiletries: can be donated to homeless shelters

Craft items: can be taken to local schools and playgroups

Linens (towels, sheets, pillows, and duvets): can be donated to
animal shelters, boarding kennels, or homeless shelters

Coat hangers: can be taken to your local dry cleaners

"Absorb what is useful. Discard what is not. Add what is uniquely your own."

– BRUCE LEE

NOT ALL CLUTTER IS JUNK

The whole act of decluttering your house may seem a little heartless, but we're all human and we all have treasured mementos. You don't need to turn yourself into a robot, instead pack your keepsakes in a special box rather than leaving them scattered about the house.

"Putting off an easy thing makes it hard. Putting off a hard thing makes it impossible."

– GEORGE CLAUDE LORIMER

CLIPBOARDS
FOR FILING

Consider using color-coded clipboards as part of your household filing system. Hang a bunch on the wall (having painted the clips different colors) and then categorize in a way that works for your household. As bills, invitations and other paperwork flows in, just clip it to the corresponding board.

"Doing just a little bit during the time we have available puts you that much further ahead than if you took no action at all."

– BYRON PULSIFER

SET GOALS

Before you get started on any tidying and organizing project,
make a plan. No matter how many rooms or how much clutter
you have to get through, start with specific goals. Set attainable
completion dates for each phase of your clean up to keep
motivation levels high.

ANOTHER WAY TO CUT DOWN ON YOUR PAPER CLUTTER

Use wipe-clean whiteboards to write shopping lists, to-do lists, or weekly planners. Frame them with ornate picture frames, so they look attractive as well as being incredibly useful.

STORAGE HACK #33

Clear your kitchen countertops by using a cake stand to hold olive oil, salt, pepper and other frequently used seasonings.

ORGANIZE YOUR FRIDGE

Just as there should be a home for everything in your house, so should there be a place for everything in your fridge. For example, put the butter, cheese, and eggs on the top shelf, milk and juice on the middle shelf, raw meats on the bottom shelf, vegetables in the vegetable box. Whatever system you create, stick to it and you will always be able to find things easily.

"Once you master time, you will understand how true it is that most people overestimate what they can accomplish in a year — and underestimate what they can achieve in a decade!"

– TONY ROBBINS

OUTSOURCE IT

Utilize out-of-house resources to cut down on the number of things entering your home. For example, borrow books from the library instead of buying them, rent tools for home DIY and garden jobs, download films and music instead of buying DVDs, Blu-rays, or CDs.

"To think too long about doing a thing often becomes its undoing."

– EVA YOUNG